T0379154

BE YOUR OWN BOSS

PLAN A BAKE SALE

STEPHANE HILLARD

PowerKiDS
press™

New York

Published in 2021 by The Rosen Publishing Group, Inc.
29 East 21st Street, New York, NY 10010

Copyright © 2021 by The Rosen Publishing Group, Inc.

All rights reserved. No part of this book may be reproduced in any form without permission in writing from the publisher, except by a reviewer.

First Edition

Portions of this work were originally authored by Emma Carlson Berne and published as *Run Your Own Bake Sale*. All new material in this edition authored by Stephane Hillard.

Editor: Elizabeth Krajnik
Book Design: Reann Nye

Photo Credits: Cover Inti St Clair/Getty Images; series art stas11/Shutterstock.com; p. 5 Michael Bezjian/WireImage/Getty Images; p. 7 Lordn/Shutterstock.com; p. 9 EasterBunny/Shuttertock.com; p. 11 MSPhotographic/Shutterstock.com; p. 13 Monkey Business Images/Shutterstock.com; p. 15 Hero Images/Getty Images; p. 17 kate_sept2004/E+/Getty Images; p. 19 Jose Luis Pelaez Inc/DigitalVision/Getty Images; p. 21 M_a_y_a/E+/Getty Images, p. 22 Mark Edward Atkinson/Tracey Lee/Getty Images.

Cataloging-in-Publication Data

Names: Hillard, Stephane.
Title: Plan a bake sale / Stephane Hillard.
Description: New York : PowerKids Press, 2021. | Series: Be your own boss | Includes glossary and index.
Identifiers: ISBN 9781725318939 (pbk.) | ISBN 9781725318953 (library bound) | ISBN 9781725318946 (6 pack)
Subjects: LCSH: Baking–Juvenile literature. | Baked products–Juvenile literature. | Fund raising–Juvenile literature. | Home-based businesses–Juvenile literature.
Classification: LCC TX683.H55 2021 | DDC 664'.752–dc23

Manufactured in the United States of America

Some of the images in this book illustrate individuals who are models. The depictions do not imply actual situations or events.

CPSIA Compliance Information: Batch #CSPK20. For Further Information contact Rosen Publishing, New York, New York at 1-800-237-9932.

CONTENTS

BECOMING AN ENTREPRENEUR 4

SUPPLY AND DEMAND 6

CREATING A BUSINESS PLAN 8

EXPENSES AND BUDGETING 10

THE IMPORTANCE OF ADVERTISING . 12

HIRING HELPERS 14

BUYING SUPPLIES 16

BAKE SALE DAY! 20

BUSINESS CHECKLIST 22

GLOSSARY 23

INDEX 24

WEBSITES 24

BECOMING AN ENTREPRENEUR

An entrepreneur is a person who starts a business and is willing to possibly lose money in order to make money. Entrepreneurs are hardworking and organized people who come up with solutions to problems—and they love being their own boss. However, you don't have to be an adult to be an entrepreneur. Plenty of kids are entrepreneurs too!

This book will show you the steps to follow to plan and start your own business, including addressing your community's needs, making a business plan, creating a **budget**, advertising, and more. In time, you'll be able to enjoy your business's **profits**.

When Alina Morse was just seven years old, she came up with the idea to make tooth-friendly lollipops. From there, her company ZolliCandy was born. Today, Morse's original product, Zollipops, are sold online and in more than 7,500 stores!

SUPPLY AND DEMAND

The purpose of a business is to provide a product or service for people. Your business should fulfill a need or a want in your community. Make a list of products or services you think you could provide. Then do some **research**. You can avoid **competition** by choosing a product or service that isn't already being provided.

Running bake sales could be a great business for you. Everyone likes to eat, so you have a built-in need already. You can sell your baked goods at school or at sporting events. A local craft show would also be a good place to have your bake sale!

GOOD BUSINESS

Toward the end of your bake sale, you can sell whatever's left at a **discount** so that you don't waste any product. This way you're still making money on something that would otherwise have to be thrown away.

If you enjoy baking, running bake sales might be the right business for you! This allows you to get paid for something you actually like doing!

CREATING A BUSINESS PLAN

Before you have your bake sale, you'll need to create a business plan. This plan outlines where, when, and how you'll run your business. First, decide where to hold your bake sale.

Next, decide when you want to hold your sale. Give yourself enough time to shop for ingredients and make your baked goods. The best time to have a bake sale is when people are hungry.

Finally, think about what supplies you'll need to run your business. Make sure you have a list of what you have and what you need to buy, rent, or borrow.

GOOD BUSINESS

Once you decide where you'll hold your bake sale, you'll want to get **permission** from the person in charge of that place and ask whether there's a fee to use the space.

Your business plan should include all the supplies you'll need, such as cookie cutters, a rolling pin, pans, mixing bowls, the ingredients for your baked goods, and much more. Make sure you don't forget anything!

EXPENSES AND BUDGETING

All businesses have expenses, which are costs that arise throughout the course of doing business. Creating a budget for your bake sale business will allow you to keep track of what you're spending money on. Your expenses will help you figure out how much you should charge for your baked goods.

After you've created your budget, check how much money you have saved. Do you have enough saved to run your business for the first month? If you don't have enough, you'll need to borrow some, most likely from your parents. Then you'll need to make a plan to repay them.

GOOD BUSINESS

You can avoid borrowing money by making an educated guess about how much profit you'll make. Then, you can borrow the smallest amount possible. However, make sure you budget a little extra for expenses you didn't plan for.

A good way to save money is to choose simple recipes, such as banana bread. These may take less time to make, have fewer or simpler ingredients, and may not require special processes or tools.

THE IMPORTANCE OF ADVERTISING

Advertising is how you'll let people know that you're planning to hold a bake sale. You can advertise by telling people, which is called word-of-mouth advertising, or by making eye-catching and **informative** flyers and signs. It's a good idea to work the cost of these supplies into your budget. You can hand out your flyers to your classmates or neighbors and post signs around your neighborhood or at school.

Your flyers and signs should include the date, time, and location of your bake sale. You can also include what types of baked goods you'll be selling.

GOOD BUSINESS

Word-of-mouth advertising is free. At school, you can ask your principal to **mention** your bake sale during announcements. During sporting events, you can ask the announcer to mention your bake sale during a timeout or at halftime.

You can ask your parents to post an ad on their social media pages, such as Facebook or Instagram. You can also ask them to help you create an event page for your bake sale.

HIRING HELPERS

Hiring people to help you run your bake sale business may make things easier for you. You might need help shopping for supplies, baking your goodies, setting up and taking down your sale, and selling your baked goods.

Ask your friends if they want to be **employees**. You can pay them a flat fee or you can pay them by the hour. The money you'll pay your employees will come out of the money you make from your bake sale. With help, you can run a larger bake sale, make more money, and still make the same—or even more—profits!

Having a friend help you with your bake sale may make things more fun for you. You'll have someone to talk to if sales are slow and it'll make the time pass by quicker.

BUYING SUPPLIES

Buying supplies will probably be your biggest expense. If you buy too many supplies and don't use them all, you'll have wasted money. This will cut into your profits.

Carefully plan out what ingredients you'll need. Keep enough on hand that you can remake something if it doesn't turn out right the first time. Make sure you have the right tools, such as measuring cups and spoons, cookie cutters, a rolling pin, and baking pans.

You should also consider whether you'd like to display your baked goods on plates or if you'll package them individually. These things cost money too.

GOOD BUSINESS

Using fresh ingredients will make your baked goods taste better. However, you don't want to buy fresh ingredients in bulk because they may spoil. For ingredients such as milk and eggs, only buy a little more than you need.

To save money, you can ask your parents or neighbors if you can borrow or rent some of their baking pans.

Don't forget to buy your advertising supplies. Buying some of these things online or in bulk may save you money. You'll also need a large table and a cash box to hold change and the money you earn. Don't forget coins and small bills to make change. You can get these from the bank.

Unless you live close enough to a store to ride your bike or walk, you'll need to ask an adult to take you shopping. Be sure to ask politely and with enough advance notice that the adult can find the time to do this for you.

Keep track of how much money you've spent on supplies and how much money you've borrowed. This will make it easier to know how much profit you're making.

BAKE SALE DAY!

Now that you've created your business plan, made a budget, advertised, and baked your goodies, you're ready for business! Gather your baked goods and other supplies and ask an adult to give you a ride to your bake sale.

Start setting up an hour or two before your sale. Tape a sign to the front of your table with the name of the bake sale and hours. Keep track of each purchase and count your money at the end. Subtract the amount you had in your cash box at the beginning of the day from the money you earned from the bake sale. How much money did you make? That is your profit!

Congratulations! You've successfully run your own bake sale! Now you can enjoy your profits!

BUSINESS CHECKLIST

- Address a community need
- Create a business plan
- Create a budget
- Purchase supplies for baking, advertising, and bake sale
- Advertise your bake sale
- Bake your goodies
- Set up your bake sale
- Get down to business
- Enjoy the profits

GLOSSARY

budget: A plan used to decide the amount of money that can be spent and how it will be spent.

competition: A person or group you're trying to succeed against.

discount: Cheaper than usual.

employee: A person who is paid to work for another.

informative: Giving knowledge or information.

mention: To talk about, write about, or refer to something especially in a brief way.

permission: The approval of a person in authority.

profit: The gain after all the expenses are subtracted from the total money received.

research: Careful study that is done to find and report new knowledge about something.

INDEX

A
advertising, 4, 12, 18, 20, 22

B
budget, 4, 10, 12, 20, 22
business plan, 4, 8, 9, 20, 22

C
competition, 6

E
employee, 14
entrepreneur, 4
expenses, 10, 16

F
flyer, 12

I
ingredients, 8, 9, 11, 16

M
money, 4, 6, 10, 11, 14, 16, 17, 18, 19, 20
Morse, Alina, 5

P
product, 5, 6
profit, 4, 10, 14, 16, 19, 21, 22

R
recipes, 11

S
service, 6
social media, 13
supplies, 8, 9, 12, 14, 16, 18, 19, 20, 22

Z
ZolliCandy, 5
Zollipops, 5

WEBSITES

Due to the changing nature of Internet links, PowerKids Press has developed an online list of websites related to the subject of this book. This site is updated regularly. Please use this link to access the list:
www.powerkidslinks.com/byoboss/bakesale